A Recipe for Water

GILLIAN CLARKE was born in Cardiff in 1937, and now lives in Ceredigion. A poet, writer, playwright and tutor on the M.Phil in Creative Writing at the University of Glamorgan, she is also president of Tŷ Newydd, the writers' centre in North Wales which she co-founded in 1990. In 2008 she was appointed the National Poet of Wales. Carcanet publish her *Collected Poems* and *Selected Poems*.

Also by Gillian Clarke from Carcanet Press

Collected Poems
The King of Britain's Daughter
Five Fields
Selected Poems
Making the Beds for the Dead
At the Source

GILLIAN CLARKE

A Recipe for Water

CARCANET

First published in Great Britain in 2009 by
Carcanet Press Limited
Alliance House
Cross Street
Manchester M2 7AQ

A CIP catalogue record for this book is available from the British Library
ISBN 978 1 85754 988 1

The publisher acknowledges financial assistance from Arts Council England

Typeset by XL Publishing Services, Tiverton
Printed and bound in England by SRP Ltd, Exeter

For David

Acknowledgements

Acknowledgements are due to the following publications where some of these poems, versions or translations of them, first appeared: *Planet*; *The New Welsh Review*; *Orbis*; *Touchstone*; *Taliesin*; *A470*; *Magma*; *Journal of the Academy of Social Studies* (June 2008); *Welsh and Proud Of It* (Pont Books 2007); *Poems of Love and Longing* (Pont Books 2008); *Branch Lines: Edward Thomas and Contemporary Poetry* (ed. Guy Cuthbertson and Lucy Newlyn, Enitharmon 2007). ''Sgwarnog' and 'Shepherd' first appeared in *At the Source* (Carcanet 2008).

I am grateful to the following for commissioning some of these poems: Ledbury Festival 2005; Bath Festival of Literature, 2008; Eisteddfod Genedlaethol Caerdydd 2008; Green Bay Television; *The Verb*, BBC Radio 3; *Woman's Hour*, BBC Radio 4; the Royal Society of Architects in Wales; Theatr Arad Goch; the Bevan Foundation; St Fagans Folk Museum; the Royal Commission for Ancient Monuments; Galeri, Caernarfon. Thanks are due to Cardiff City Council and the Academi for my year as Capital Poet in 2005, which prompted the City poems; the Sociology Department of Cardiff University for commissioning poems for the Futures Conference, 2005; Poetry Live and the British Council for the week spent in Mumbai, 2007; the Academi and the Welsh Assembly Government for opportunities and commissions arising from the post of National Poet for Wales.

Contents

First Words

The alphabet of a house – air,
breath, the creak of the stair.
Downstairs the grown-ups' hullabaloo,
or their hush as you fall asleep.

You're learning the language: the steel slab
of a syllable dropped at the docks; the two-beat word
of the Breaksea lightship; the golden sentence
of a train crossing the viaduct.

Later, at Fforest, all the words are new.
You are your grandmother's Cariad, not Darling.
Tide and current are *llanw, lli*.
The waves repeat their *ll-ll-ll* on sand.

Over the sea the starlings come in paragraphs.
She tells you a tale of a girl and a bird,
reading it off the tide in lines of longhand
that scatter to bits on the shore.

The sea turns its pages, speaking in tongues.
The stories are yours, and you are the story.
And before you know it you'll know what comes
from air and breath and off the page is all

you'll want, like the sea's jewels in your hand,
and the soft mutations of sea washing on sand.

A Pocket Dictionary

'Geiriadur Llogell Cymraeg a Saesoneg', 1861

Fifty years. His handwriting, his name, address.
Richards' Pocket Dictionary. 1861.
My father's fingerprints. Mine over his.
I look up a word, as I've so often done,
without a thought beyond the page, the word.
Now syllables flock like a whirr of redwings
over the field of my mind. Here the world
began, and then is now. I am searching
for definitions, ambiguities, way
down through the strata, topsoil, rubble,
a band of clay, an inch or so of gravel,
for a particular carbon-dated day,
a seepage in the earth, a gleam of meaning,
a sudden uprise of remembering.

Glas y Dorlan

So he said, 'Let's begin by naming the creatures.'
Once in the Brecon Beacons we stopped for a picnic
where the river roared headstrong down the mountain.

A sudden electric blue, a shock through the heart.
What was that? A bird diving faster than gravity
into the pool and up with a fish in its beak.

He spoke its name, doused in the shout of the falls.
Fisher-bird, King of the Water, *Pioden y Dŵr*,
Glas y Dorlan. Blue-by-the Riverbank.

Not

My mother, child of a tenant farm,
learned her place from the landlord's man,
his word 'Welsh' snapped, cutting, curt,
a word that called her 'stranger'.

So my mother would not say the word.
but spat it out like a curse,
a bitterness to be rid of,
to be scoured from her mouth.

My mother's word didn't sound
like the name for a people,
for 'us', for belonging,
for a language older than legend;

or like Nain on the farm, tucking me in
with a prayer and 'Nos da, Cariad',
or calling the hens in the morning, her voice
all cluck and chuckle like scattering corn;

or my father passing the time with stories
as we drove to the sea, teaching me words,
the 'gw' and 'w' of wind and water,
the *ll-ll-ll* of waves on the shore.

Otter

Little water-dog. They almost caught her –
the surface closing over
as the sounding rings of a splash
smashed the moonlit water.

It made its mark on the shore –
paw-print of an otter
and the peeled skull of a frog
just after the slaughter.

Frog caught on the quiet, quartered,
till the skull was a moon
as silvery clean as a spoon
but colder, whiter.

Father and daughter
heard the frog cry '*Broga. Broga.*'
Then '*Dŵr. Dŵr,*' said water
as it swallowed the otter.

The Fox and the Girl

Once her father came home with a fox cub
in his coat pocket. Lost in the city,
shivering in rubbish outside the pub.
the colour of conkers and as pretty

as a puppy, its teeth like needles.
It hissed in her arms, but she wheedled
to keep it. When it bit her she cried
for her bloody hand, and she cried

when he said, 'Mae'n wyllt. It's a wild
animal, not a pet for a child.'
She could feel its life, its warm fur,
its quick heart beating against her,

and she hurt for its animal mystery,
for the vanishing story of a girl
and a fox lost for words
in the secret forest.

'Sgwarnog

'Tell me the names for the hare!'
' *'Sgwarnog* for its long ears.
Cochen for its red-brown fur.
Ceinach for its intricate criss-cross track.
Cath Eithin, Cath y Mynydd,
Cat of the gorse, of the mountain.'

There, alive, over the hedge,
in the field by the cliff-path,
one of her kindle, her kittens,
a leveret alone, stone-still in its cwtsh
till she comes at dusk to suckle it,
murmuring mother tongue.

Nettles

for Edward Thomas

No old machinery, no tangled chains
of a harrow locked in rust and rising grasses,
nor the fallen stones of ancient habitation
where nettles feed on what we leave behind.
Nothing but a careless compost heap
warmed to a simmer of sickly pungency,
lawn clippings we never moved, but meant to,

and can't, now, because nettles have moved in,
and it's your human words inhabit this.
And, closer, look! The stems lean with the weight,
the young of peacock butterflies, just hatched,
their glittering black spines and spots of pearl.
And I want to say to the dead, look what a poet sings
to life: the bite of nettles, caterpillars, wings.

A T-Mail to Keats

Dear John Keats,

I write to suggest that poets never die.
The old poetry drums in the living tongue,
phrase and image like bright stones in the stream
of common speech, its cadences a beat
that resonates as long as language lives.

I want to talk with you of the new nature,
of your grief at science for *unweaving the rainbow*.
But listen to the poetry of light,
the seven colours of coronas, glories, haloes,
how no two people see the same rainbow.

Oh, soon may science solve time's mystery!
Already words can take flight from our hands
over land and continents and seas,
with the small sigh of a shooting star.
If words can cross space, why not time?

In hope, I send this message into space.
May we meet over a verse, a glass
or two of the *blushful Hippocrene,*
a draught of vintage that hath been
cooled a long age in the deep-delved earth
in the ice-house of our refrigerator.

In esteem.
GC

Fflam

for Gwyn Thomas

For so long a flame has flickered
at the cromlech, at the crossroad,
in encampment, hovel and castle,
in the courts of minor princes.

Song by firelight, gleam of a sword,
the quiver of a harp string,
reflections in the faces
of those tranced by listening.

The word is out. It crosses
centuries, each one a torch,
every syllable a heartbeat,
every song a torch in the dark.

Gwyn, we meet at the ford,
to speak in tongues,
to pass on simple truth,
to torch the lies, the weasel words,

burn off the fog of politics
with poetry's flame,
to illuminate
the mind's manuscript.

The Ledbury Muse

7.7.05

A blackbird cuts a dash straight down Church Lane,
picks scraps from the Market Hall. Again, again
he skims the cobbles in the rising sun
too quick to glimpse the fabulous flaw, his one
rumoured white feather. Muse of the streets and yards,
old as the town, rough scruff of a bird,
five hundred years ago his voice was heard
by drovers, strolling players, itinerant bards.
He is silent now. This songless July morning
before the news breaks, the blackbird's lost his voice.
Rumour, footsteps, voices sound the space.
It's our turn now to hold our ground with warning.
To cry out against terror is what poetry's for,
to admit our one white feather, our fatal, human flaw.

A Recipe for Water

for Sujata Bhatt

Fifty feet down
water flows in the dark.
Rains that spent history
seeping page by page
through the strata,

run black in the aquifers
to rise bringing their gift,
the formula like a spell,
a gulp of cold that flares
at the touch of light.

Calcium, Magnesium, Potassium, Sodium,
Chloride, Sulphate, Nitrate, Iron.

Sip this, the poetry of stone,
a mineral Latin in our blood, our bone.

★

The first word for water.
Wysg. Usk. Esk. Wye.
First clicks, clucks, monosyllables,
sibilant spillings in imitation
of the sound of all that shining.

Or the sound of thirst,
the suck and lap as a small pool ripples
in the cup of two hands,
an ecstasy of spill on skin, hair, mouth,
drops beading the dust.

★

The second word for water.
Dûfr. Dûr. Dyfroedd. Dover.

Imagine the moment a man,
a woman singing in a dark age,

gazed from those chalk heights
at the vast and broken seas

and sang this word, song and word
on the tongue, in the throat,

finding a name for an element.
Everywhere on earth, the first human word

as small as the single drop of rain
a blackbird needs to begin a dawn song.

★

That drop on the tongue
was the first word in the world
head back, eyes closed, mouth open
to drink the rain
wysg, uisc, dûr, hudra, aqua, agua, eau, wasser

★

You imagine me writing in the falling rain,
rain on the roof, writing in whispers
on the slates' lectern,
rain spelling out each syllable
like a child learning to read.

But day after day
no huff of rain
on the roof,
frost a dry breath on grass.

The trees stop drinking,
their secret roots a delta under the earth,
their branches against the winter sky
waiting for spring to make a move.

Rain must relearn how to sound.
March rain must learn to be wild,
to fill the mouth of the west wind
with salt skinned off the sea.

So long the Atlantic has waited,
dragging its anchor.
These dry days and nights
I feel its weight like gravity.

*

Weeks of journeys into frozen England.
One dusk, the north-bound Pendolino
leans out for the dance across the Midlands,
creeping so slowly between claypits,

canals and the backs of houses,
that there's time for a woman's hands
in a lit kitchen to turn on a tap
and fill a bowl with what I know

is my sweet mountain water
brought all the way by gravity.

White

After the theatre, stirred by song and story,
we watch the winter stars from the balcony.

Five floors down from our room in the hotel,
two ice-floes in flux on flow. Each candela

is a mute swan asleep, as white, as luminous
on the black waters of the bay as ice.

Stilled at the edge of the Severn's turbulence
and the tangled waters of two river currents,

their whiteness the definition of lumen,
swans paired for life, a cob and his pen,

wings and necks folded in one dream,
and all the colours of white, which only seem,

Sujata, the very opposite of the blackness
of your black squirrel in Caracas,

but are the same, the one
white rainbow, black, one spectrum.

★

All the spare light in the world is stored
in the folded wings of a pair of sleeping swans,

all the world's spare water stacked miles deep
in the waking ice of the glacier.

The last star dissolves at the lost edge of the moon
afloat on blue like Arctic ice, loosening.

★

At last a change in the weather.
Frost gives up its grip,
ice eases in the bones of trees.
There is movement in the air,
the Atlantic on the wind's breath,
a touch of rain beginning.

Severn

A Barge on the Severn

after a painting by Colin Jones (1928–1967)

Where river becomes estuary
before losing its name to the sea,
in water angled by a harbour wall,
on the tilt of the tide's rise and fall
between mudflats, saltmarsh and flood plain,
a boat with the sea in its lap, or rain.

He could have put the river to bed,
baled out the barge, drowned to its gunwale
in flood, in the hope of letting it float.
But he caught the hour and held it,
the cruciform spars of the stern where light
and a salt wind off the channel

still make its lost sail snap in a cross wind,
and the colours brought home in his mind
– red flaking and faded to rose,
and the blue-green of water – have held
forty years, while he, the barge, a particular
hour, timbers, molecules, pigment, particles,

are swept with the soils and silts of Pumlimon
to become the Severn.

Source

After hours plodding uphill in something between
rain and an Atlantic haar, we have come to this:
two thousand feet above the Irish Sea,
a pane of ice, and a muscle of pooling water,

Pumlimon, where five rivers rise, a squelch
of tussocky bog, and the cairn, Garn-fach Bugeilyn,
where story tells us Cai and Bedwyr stood
'in the highest wind in the world'.

We witness a birth, uncertain of what is born,
though we see it's alive, its pulsing placenta,
Hafren, Sabrina, gurgling out of the earth,
headwaters of a stream that will augment

to a headlong hurtling force ready to swallow
Vyrnwy, Stour, Teme, Avon, Afon and Wye,
to bring mountain waters to lap at the thresholds
of cities, to bear off the dead, to shove its way

through limestone in the gorge at Ironbridge,
to be fluent under bridges, to open its hands
letting its multiple muscular waters spread,
to become the estuary, to be lost in the sea.

Sabrina

There is a gentle nymph not far from hence
That with moist curb sways the smooth Severn stream.
Sabrina is her name, a virgin pure

Milton, 'Comus'

Before history there was mythology.
Fingerprinted between the strata of story
Is the human sign. We make a guess
At who they were, and where and why it was.
How the daughter of faithless Locrinus drowned
Between an Ice Age and the Age of Stone
To become the river-goddess, a curb in the river.
Today in these fast waters you might glimpse
In the sway of the currents the white limbs
Of a girl caught in a shoal of silvers
Turning and turning in the turbulence
Among migrating salmon, sewin, elvers,

Lampreys, eels taking their ancient water-roads
Under the shadows of thousands of homing birds.

Ice

stopped the throat of the Severn
in the last Ice Age.
so it slept three thousand years,
locked in a frozen lake,

thawed slowly,
built power
beyond Wenlock Edge,
turned south-east,

forced a six mile gorge through rock
at Ironbridge, let loose
the coal, iron, limestone, clay,
that would change the world.

Tide

Lured by the very thought of it, forty-nine feet,
the second highest rise and fall in the world.
Some mornings full to the brim, it slapped and curled
over the prom, and by evening was so far out
you couldn't tell sea from pools, pebbles, mudflats,
wet acres of seaweed, shells, old rope, bird-bones,
fishing lines hooked in the silt, worm-casts, stones,
streams of ebbing water flashing with light.
Once, on a strange beach, the Severn turned on us.
It surged thundering up the steep sand,
carried and cast us ashore like detritus
then tried to drag us back on retreating waters,
as when the sea-king stole the old man's daughters.

Bore

The sea charges in
against the outpour
of a big, bold river.
no holds barred.

So a water-dragon is born.
A self-powering soliton
heaves upstream,
rearing its crested head,

past cathedrals, towns,
a seven foot wave
rolling up-country
where no wave should be.

It rips out river banks,
nudges a stone from the stanchion
of a bridge,
sweeps footpaths away,

carries off cars,
the carcass of a sheep,
tons of old red sandstone,
and surfers hitching a ride.

Barrage

No entry to 68,000 wintering birds:
dunlin back from Scandinavia to their usual place,
the greatest gathering of shelduck in Europe,
no entry to Bewick's swan,
pintail, wigeon, redshank.

No entry to the breeding grounds
for curlew, oystercatcher.
No entry to 30,000 homing salmon
to great shoals of shad, lampreys, and sewin
to spawn in the Usk and the Wye.

No exit to millions of eels and elvers
as they swim down river to the spawning grounds.
No entry when they return in spring.

Migrations

Signals
between a weather satellite
wavering among the steady stars
and seven swans tagged with transmitters,
asleep on a lake in southern Finland.

First light. Bewick's and Whooper swans
wheel off the water, beating west,
the Russian Arctic tundra out of mind,
their future the washy estuaries
of Severn, Dyfi, Neb or Ouse.

It's nothing new, on wing, on foot,
the hungry take to the roads of a restless earth,
in flight from famine, slaughter, war,
on ancient journeys across seas, deserts,
across the latitudes and longitudes.

But this is new, intimate, tracking
the secret flight of a Bewick's swan,
its heartbeat in my hand
as it homes a thousand miles,
to winter on wetlands in Wales.

I fly with it, imagining space
beating with luminous wings:
satellites, angels, souls,
the seven ghosts of Concorde
blowing the firmament,

the world's roads dark
with human travellers,
each caravan of hunger
a mythic journey to an inn,
in want of shelter, water, bread.

Mumbai

Man in a Shower

He is beyond glass, wrapped in a waterfall,
undressing himself of the city's dirt, his arms
tearing the cawl of water to be born afresh
in the heat of the morning. Man alone in his shower,
absorbed in sunlight and water, he accepts
the gift of a running tap on the highway embankment
letting its bright rope run through his hands.

Today he is rich. Today he will not want
for work, or food, or shelter, or respect.
His two hands are a funnel pouring silver
over his hair, his chest, his human shoulders
with their broken angel wings, the beads of his spine,
the ropes of his arms, thighs, the pearl knobs
of his wrists, each foot lifted for blessing.

Rajendra revs, easing us onto the highway
into the rumpus of car horns, filth, burning
rubber and air, a river of metal and oil
eternally choked in a gorge, leaving behind
in the teeming city the image of a man
in the pleasure of his morning ablutions,
clean and blameless as a newborn.

At the Banganga Tank

On the steps of the tank a woman washes herself
dipping jug after jug in the blue of the pool,
her sari the colour of her skin. She is moulded

in water and light, clean and cool
on the steps, a woman of gold
pouring and filling the cast of herself.

A naked child stands, eyes closed tight,
robed in a gown of foam
as soap is rinsed from her hair.

They wash themselves in the evening light
by the water, laving from body and soul
the dirt and disease you can smell in the stagnant air.

We stroll the path round the pool.
Women sit on the steps, they greet us,
their children wave and blow kisses.

An old woman folds her hands like prayer,
inclines her head and touches her brow
with her fingertips, and teaches me how.

They are taking the air
by water so cerulean blue
it is surely toxic.

In the Taj

I love the holy ritual in the loos,
especially at the Taj Mahal Hotel.

I work it out: none must touch a handle, a tap,
or anything at all with tainted hands.

A smiling priestess with a white cloth
goes in, comes out, then bids me enter.

When I emerge she is there, turning the tap for me,
filling my palm with soap, folding my hands in my own white towel.

A woman gestures her away and turns the tap herself
with her unwashed Anglo-Saxon white-woman hands,

rich enough to holiday in such a place,
too illiterate to read between the lines.

Laundry

Outside the shacks by the Tulsi Pipe Road
the women are laundering rainbows,
heaving cloth into tubs, load after load.
They lift and twist red, indigo, yellow
with their thin bangled arms,
as our foremothers might have done
in a mountain stream or tarn,
or a pure spring by the road.

They must wring every rag
for its strings of water-jewels,
to be saved and re-used.
They drape their glories like flags
over dipping wires and trees
dirtied at once in a lift of the breeze
by road-dust, particulates of petrol, diesel.
They will sleep dazed by the fumes.

Hands

Rajendra drives us across the city.
When we're stalled or creeping in traffic
hands crowd like leaves glued to glass.
A mother signs hunger, holds out her baby.
A girl with a twisted mouth.
A leper with a bucket hooked on his stump.

We wind down the window two inches,
and hand bananas, spring water.
Clean nourishing things,
not money for powdered milk
to mix with polluted water
that poisons their babies.

Ahead a child in a white dress
is spun like a struck bird
as a car speeds away at the lights.
She's left reeling and angry,
collecting herself for the next chance,
a bird spinning in the slipstream

of a car, the wake of a ferry,
on the runway as the jet takes off,
blood on its feathers.
one wing lifting in the wind.

Post Script

Grieve for the broken city,
for the man borne in the doorman's arms
to a golden luggage cart

for the gentle women in the loos,
their smiles, their immaculate towels,
their hands

for the waiter killed as he turned
in the shocked restaurant,
a silver tray on his palm

for the black hearts of boys
in a fever of power,
for their mothers, their fathers

for the beggar child in a world torn
like a shot bird,
still shaking

Glacier

The miles–deep Greenland glacier's lost its grip,
sliding nine miles a year towards the sea
on its own melt–water. As, forty years ago,
the slag–heap, loosened by a slip
of rain–swollen mountain streams, suddenly
gave with a roar, a down–hurtling flow
of spoil taking a primary school.
crushing the children. The century of waste
has burned a hole in the sky over the Pole.
Oh, science, with your tricks and alchemies,
chain the glacier with sun and wind and tide,
rebuild the gates of ice, halt melt and slide,
freeze the seas, stay the floe and the flux
for footfall of polar bear and Arctic fox.

The Reader's Digest Atlas of the World

1986 edition

My favourite page, the map of the world's currents.
The North Atlantic Gyre marked with red arrows
where the Gulf Stream signs its hot name in the sea.

We live by temperate waters because of this
fragile coincidence, moon–pull and turning Earth,
a lion-breath from Africa, the Gulf of Mexico,

a golden road bearing north a stream
of tropical heat to meet the Arctic cold
and fall, for all we know, five thousand fathoms

then turn, cooling, taking the usual route
among the multiple currents of the ocean,
a cold blue undulation arrowing south.

City

First, perhaps, we should view it across water,
passing two islands on a surging tide –
just short of the greatest rise and fall in the world.

Our ship would pitch where the sea wrestles the Severn,
muscular with rain from heart and hinterland,
sullen with slag and silky river silts.

Whoever they are, whatever tongue they speak,
from what continent, what distant island,
they crossed an ocean to help make the city.

Rounding the headland a hundred years ago,
most of them frozen, feverish, seasick, heartsick,
rolling up channel into the throat of the Severn,

they'd see the clock tower of the City Hall,
rumoured white buildings between broad avenues,
parkland and pleasure grounds beside the Taff.

For me it was 'let's pretend', lying awake
to the blink and sob of the Breaksea lightship,
my trip on the paddle steamer to Ilfracombe

a voyage from Africa, the *Cardiff Queen*
smashing the evening sea to smithereens,
a coming home made glamorous by dream

to a city we'd imagined into being.
Seeing's believing, believing's seeing.

Afon Tâf

Before river turned reflective,
a tremble of terraces
like jugs on a dresser,
a flight of bridges,

it was mountain rain,
mud-puddle, melt-water,
up-bubbling springs
on Penyfan and Corn-Du.

It was reservoir and weir,
Tâf Fechan, Tâf Fawr,
shouldering the dam
with the sway of its weight.

It was white water falling,
combed by the flood-gates.
It was Nant Ffrwd, Nant Morlais,
Nant Rhydycar.

Before river was glass
at the lip of the Severn
featherweight with swans,
sails and white hotels,

before it dozed in the Bay
it was wind and wilderness,
dipper and kingfisher,
crow and kite –

gwynt a gwylltineb,
'deryn du'r dŵr,
glas y dorlan,
brân a barcud.

Architect

E.A.Rickards (1872–1920)

Such a tonnage of Portland stone,
shipped to a coal town as the century turned.
Luminous, Jurassic, pure as stacked ice,
and marble from Sienna unloaded in the dirt
beside the black, black coal that paid for it.

Oh, to have been there, a hundred years ago,
Law Courts and City Hall complete,
flanking an avenue of sapling elms
among those sixty empty parkland acres,
there at the birth of a city;

to have stood that night with the young architect,
self-taught, flamboyant, garrulous,
in love with high Edwardian Baroque;
to have shared his grand romantic gesture,
bringing a friend to view his work by moonlight,

to see his buildings carved from ice,
the clock tower's pinnacle, the clock
counting its first hours towards us,
when moonlight through long windows of the marble hall
cast pages yet to be written.

Coins

Stalled in Kingsway traffic, engine idle,
watching for peacocks and the grey friar's ghost,
I remember the diving boys, the water-course lost
under the hum and cumber, the old canal

scuttling in its culvert, covert, echoing
slaps of rat-shadow and the shout
of marble boys, or boys as brown as trout,
their skinny shoulder blades like broken wings.

They dived for pennies from the parapet
a life ago, falling through green light
with a gasp, to surface, blowing water,
shaking their otter heads, coins bright

on their palms. Down there in the filth and cold
lies, dated like a journal, my lost gold.

Llandâf Cathedral

Before the saints, Dyfrig, Teilo, Eiddogwy;
before the bishops, the builders and stonemasons;
before artists and sculptors, Rossetti, Epstein;
before music, organists and choirs;
before architects, Jasper Tudor, Wood, Seddon, Prichard, Pace;
before the poetry of psalm and hymn and common prayer;

before 'cathedral', 'architecture', 'art',
when our first house
was the great original forest,
when our ancestors walked in the aisles of trees
and gazed up into the loftiness, confused,
perhaps, by inexplicable longing;

before there was a word for wonder,
or names for stars, or footprints on the moon,
before Saint Teilo raised his church just here,
before a man looked at a tree and made a cross,
and felt the hammering rain and thought of nails,
there must have been a first creative act,

first mark, first word, first hymn to awe,
first poem with something to say of the human heart,
first vision of a building taller than the forest,
aisled, vaulted, clerestoried with sunlight, imagined
into being, because we were forest-dwellers once
and learned our metaphors from trees.

Sleepless

Ear to the wall of the night. Listen
to your blood beat in the pulse of your pillow,
the water table rising in your bones,
the future drumming the ground like a train on the track.

Out there the car parks lie like frozen lakes.
Taxis bear away the late night people
home to the suburbs and the big estates,
to blocks of flats and long Victorian terraces,
panels of coloured glass in each front door
where the light in the hall waits up late.
Home to rented rooms, cheap lodging houses,
five star hotels with their golden portals,
their whispering lifts and all-night smiles.

The hospital by the dual carriageway
is an anchored ferry glittering in the night,
attending the song and dance of birth,
death's flashing semaphore.
An ambulance waits for trouble in a lay-by.
A night nurse sheds her uniform of pity
as she turns for home. A midwife remembers
the newborn's stuttering cry, its smell of the sea.

The early hours. You dream the sleeping city
beyond blind windows. A late car passes
with a sweep of light across your bedroom wall.
You write on the dark as if it were a page,
yours the one lit window in the street.

★

Dawn moves in the eastern sky. A train ticks
over the bridge, the first bus idles from its stall,
a wheeze of cranes on all-night building sites,
the two blue notes of a police car.
First sun lights the fuse of three rivers,

touches the Old Library, the Market roof,
St John's Church, slides down Castle Street,
touches lions, lioness, lynx, bear,
seal, wolf, apes, two racoons,
seventeen animals sprawled in stone
a hundred years on the Castle wall
where the river slides under the bridge.

*

The placid face of the Bay mirrors
a dazzle of apartment blocks.
Where once the tall tides rose and fell,
are the drowned rivers,
the subway that scuttled with rats,
seepings, rumours, footsteps,
where shift workers walked under the river
to load the coal boats at Alexandra Dock
in another world a lifetime ago.

*

Dream the thrust and give of the gates,
the ooze and rush of water
the let of chains and wheels,
and underground, underwater,
under the complacent face of the bay,
the drowned sob of three rivers.

*

Footsteps in the city.
You are walking towards yourself
up Morgan's Arcade to the Hayes,
in a cathedral of shopping,

through the heave of coming and going
past the flickering computer shop
with its shining boy assistants,
the deli, the frivolous shoe-shop, the café on the corner

where over coffee women gaze into bags
rustling with tissue-wrapped secrets,
packages poked at, corners lifted
for a glimpse, a gasp of pleasure

among the necessities –
fruit from a barrow, pasta from the deli,
fish and meat from the market,
the Sunday lunch.

★

Footsteps in the city.
You see yourself in angled glass,
the gesture of a window model,
the glance of a mirror.

You walk on the dead.
Underfoot, under the streets,
lie the generations,
their absorbed faces.

★

On the all-night building sites
they erase your horizon,
break and remake it.

Buildings you knew
fall to rubble and ash
under the crush of machines,

and rising out of dust
this brash new place,
reinventing itself

in pavement cafés,
in glittering glass and steel,
in shopping, shopping, shopping

to the beat of the rapper,
to the cry of street traders,
to the *Big Issue* seller,
to the sweet voice of the violin.

Subway

A glance at the brown river,
then down, under,
through the black hole in the day,
bicycle wheels spinning into the tunnel.

The tide drums overhead,
your heart thunders.
For sixty seconds the sun
drowns in the subway,

the river, the bicycle,
the flash of daps on pedals,
Under the river you speed through terror
to smash the ring of fire,

the golden O at the tunnel's end,
to come up blinking in sunlight
in a breaker's yard of old cars,
weeds, junk, wreckage,

kittens mewing in the boots of Fords,
hens chuckling in a Morris Minor,
and ten astonished piglets in a row,
like a welcome party on a foreign shore.

All your life you'd dream that birth-journey,
the dive under the bone lintel,
like escaping a sunken ship through the eye
of a porthole sleepy with sea.

The Rising Tide

The city knows it in its bones,
in the skulls of the dead,
the murdered and the drowned
lost in river silts
with all our archaeology,
shoes, prams, plastic, supermarket trolleys,
the ribcages of boats, their cabins
locked by the weight of the sea.

There's a rumour of rising damp,
something shifting in clay foundations.
The city listens to its own heart-murmur.
a pulse of water in its arteries
unsettling settlements.
Salts bloom on basement walls.
House-walls crack in summer drought,
the heave of winter rain.

And the ordinary dead,
with their quiet histories,
will be the first to know,
six feet under in their cemeteries,
seepage sifting their bones
as the water-table rises.
When the Severn shoulders in
against outpouring Taff, Ely and Rhymney,
the streets will become a delta,
terraces afloat, reflective.

Welsh

In the city I was born in,
it reached me like a rumour:
the name of a house, a suburb,
a word in my ear,
letters in family longhand.

It came down wires,
through walls in grown-up voices,
whispered behind hands,
pencilled in the margins
of Waldo and T.H. Parry-Williams.

The new lagoon has little to say,
safe from the surges of the Severn,
but at night, on the quiet, Taff and Ely
murmur at the harbour wall,
a sob in the throat of the sea.

And here in the square, the word's on the street.
Children chatter past my pavement table
as if they own the city, as if it's ordinary
to shake the dust off a rumour,
to shimmy and shout in Welsh in a Cardiff square.

Stadium

Wing

Hare outrunning the pack.
Trick of the light.
He's not there, there,
a shouldering swerve,

foot, thigh, heart, eye,
sinew and nerve
too quick, too far
to see how, where,

with sleight of foot,
feint, flex and turn,
he dodges the charge
and breaks for the open

to a roar that enflames
the drums of his heart
and the single heart
of a multitude rising.

Number 8

And sometimes he'll slip the knot of the scrum
with the ball on his palm, and run with it
hand on heart, out of the mud and bone,

the way a lovely muscle of river
will loosen the branchy tangle
that blocks its way,

and making a break for it flow,
sleek and dangerous
over the weir.

★

The legend goes like this:
the land was cold and bare,
when its people woke to a strange new hope
and a mood of devil-may-care.

There was one with a silver boot
and one with a raptor's stare,
and all of them young and strung with steel,
ready to do and dare.

There was one with the speed of a hound
and one with the heart of a hare,
and millions to surge and urge them on
to fly on a wing and a prayer.

Mist lifted from the land,
the sun stood in the air,
when the ball sailed straight through the golden gate,
like a comet with streaming hair,

and bells rang and the people sang
and all was debonair.

Letting the Light In

Well building hath three Conditions: Commodity, Firmness and Delight.

Sir Henry Wotton, 1624

A cwtsh of a country,
houses hunkered to the hill
in heartless, one-street towns.
The et cetera of terraces
like paragraphs of longhand
in an old language.

In our town by the sea, we children
were construction workers,
clearing glades in the woods for dens,
tree-houses, bird-hides, lookouts.
We'd ease into hollow trees
and whisper in the mushroomy dark.

Till suddenly called by the distant drum of a train
we'd race breathless to the viaduct,
to take the measure of it, to shout,
to touch the train's thunder in the stones,
sound and curve diminishing arch by arch
in lapsing loops and ellipses.

It prepared us for the lofty gravity
of museum, warehouse, galleried arcades,
Victorian covered market, old library
whispering its multilingual stories,
tea and talk under trees in the open air
at the Hayes Island Snack Bar.

*

In the re-imagined nation, let's dream
a waterfront where once the coal ships docked,
leafy squares where sunlight turns, touching
stalls, strollers, street musicians, a woman
at a pavement table, steam from a white cup,
coins in the fiddler's opened case.

Let's make fine buildings, go sandalfoot
into spaces of shadows and reflections,
see what stone, steel, slate and glass,
can make out of air and water and sunlight.
Let's open the city to the light,
to commodity, firmness, delight.

House of Dreams

Oh, the lights, and the box,
and the party frocks,
and the let's pretend,
and the happy ending
that first time
at the Pantomime,
when you were seven or eight
and stayed up late.

Years later, Shakespeare,
Olivier's glittering spittle
like sparks in the spotlight,
as he whispered in your ear
how he would not weep,
how he had no more tears
to shed, and that night
you could not sleep.

In the house of mystery
your mind's blown open,
and your heart is broken
and mended and set free
by words and the way they are spoken,
by a gesture, a glance,
by music and silence,
in the house of dreams
where nothing is what it seems.

A Sonnet for Nye

London was used to trouble from the Valleys,
People who lived close, loved song and word,
Despised the big men's promises and lies.
With them the socialist vision struck a chord.
Colliers, who hated class and privilege,
Whose work was filthy, dark and perilous,
Spared a portion of their paltry wage
To pay a stricken neighbour's doctor's bills.
They sent their man to Parliament. Who dares
Wins. A fierce man with a silver tongue,
He hammered stammered words in the hallowed air
Of the House, an Olympian among them,
Stuttering his preposterous social dream
Translated from 'a little local scheme'.

Mercury

What tows it back tonight?
A bead of silver rolling among the stars,
and a jet's growl trailing behind its light.

One distant afternoon, the house in a drowse
between Hoovers and teatime, I creep in,
open his desk, slide out the drawers.

Caught from the broken barometer, harm
caged in a tobacco tin, humming, glamorous,
loose and luminous as a swarm.

The thought of it still shivers in the bone,
how it breaks into beads then shoals at the tilt of the tin.
Dangerous quicksilver. I'm alone,

while the grown-ups nap in their rooms.
Nothing to do but open things, touch the forbidden,
the whole, slow, summer afternoon.

It could get under your skin, electricity
running your veins, nerves, bones.
It could light you up like a city.

A trick of the night sky and I'm there again, taking
a tiger out of a drawer, my promise, the law,
silence, his trust, my heart, all of it breaking.

Welsh Gold

Two thousand years ago, before
he knew the word for *aurum*, *aur*,
a man was lured by a single yellow hair,
into the-gods-knew-where
of the underworld.
A sun-struck thread in rock,
filament of lightning, electric shock,
Apollo's pollens alchemised to gold.

A thousand years ago
in the scriptorium at Ystrad Flûr
a monk scribing his way across the page
a line of verse in Welsh from the Age
of Poets, heard a blackbird, clear
in the branches of an oak,
and dipping its feather in gold
touched an initial with a masterstroke.

Here, in the mine, a trace
gleams on the worked rock face
like a line of verse on the wall,
a shaft of meaning, then illegible.
The gold has all but gone, its alchemy
undone like the illusion of money.

Sunlight on the river is fools' gold.
The real stuff's stored
in human muscle, blood and bone,
and an unrecoverable hoard
slips through our hands in the sea.

Horsetail

Not a grass. Not a tree. Primitive,
leafless leftover

from forest giants that fossilised to coal,
its jointed stems rising in whorls

from coastal salts, stones, ashes, sand,
colonising ground where the trains once ran.

It feeds on rock, sucks
metals out of stone,

prospecting for wealth in the ground.
Scouring pots with it, the people found

their fingers gleamed with moon-dust, and at night
squinting by tallow candlelight

they'd grind it on a pestle
to a mess of green spittle,

the mind's fire keeping out the cold
for a few grains of gold.

Kites

A gilded initial. A pair. Four
following the combine over the barley,
a flaunt of raptors flexing tail and wings.
Flamboyance. Flames on air.

Sky and field are an open book
of land and light, flux and flair,
of air uttering in the updraughts
and slipstreams of inflexion,

of flesh-hungry angels cleaning the field
after harvest, eyes arrowing earth
for the crushed and the bloody,
for the stopped heart.

Death's Head Hawkmoth Caterpillar

How did it get here among the petunias,
under the August sun at La Guionie?
Exotic, long as your finger, speckled
and chevronned in indigo, emerald, gold,
a gaudy toy looping the flower bed,
frequenter of bittersweet, henbane, nightshade.
It will spin itself a chrysalis of spittle and clay,
dissolve, metamorphose, pupate and wait
for a rearrangement of its molecular being,
a stirring of self in the sun, a freeing.
Blind purpose sends it burrowing into the earth
for a winter waiting to be stirred by beauty,
damp wings unfolding, opening, setting it free,
the mask of death on its head from the moment of birth.

Oradour-sur-Glane

Tomorrow you will visit the village
that stopped dead
in its smoking ashes
the morning after.

Too often, in summer,
I step out of sunlight into that church,
where the molten bell's tongue
is a dumb lump in its throat.

Don't think of the children burnt in the confessional,
Don't think of the holy child in its mother's arms
that flew through the great altar window,
in a prism of stained glass and blood.

Don't think of the soldiers who raided the cellars,
fed well, drank their good wine,
pleasured themselves before sleep
dreaming of wives and lovers,

woke to a peerless summer morning,
crossed themselves, blessed
their sons, their daughters,
and set off for the slaughter.

On 10 June 1944, the inhabitants of Oradour-sur-Glane were rounded up
and murdered by the occupying SS and the village burned.

Singer

Something about its silence,
a black machine, gold finery lowered
and locked for good under the lid,
the stilled treadle, little drawers of silks,
spare needles rusting in their paper cases,

suggests a small foot rocking,
a delicate ankle bone in grey lisle
lifting and falling to an old heartbeat,
silk slipping under her hand
like the waters of the Glane beneath the bridge,

treadle and thread and woman singing
in another language sixty years ago
one warm June afternoon in Oradour,
before the sun fired the west window of the church,
before the last tram from Limoges.

Storm over Limousin

I send you a day of summer heat
from central France, breathless before storm,
then a stir of wind like the whispering of wheat
or rosaries, the black sky warm
above a million hectares of fertility.
A sudden growl of warning in the stones,
over the mountains, serpents of electricity;
in the heart, unease as old as Eden.
I send you this, shimmering over Limousin,
the sound of weighty matter heaved across
the floor of heaven, till earth is diamond,
and there signed on the road, belly up, crushed
on the road in Ségur, a snake, like lightning's memory,
someone's initial signed on an old story.

Landscape with Farm

after a painting by Evan Walters

There is always a white farm,
somewhere between you and the horizon,
a hundred fields folded under a sky
of scudding cloud. A hamlet, a church tower,
broken-backed barns and fallen walls dissolve
and light converges in one glowing gable,
the bright brow that holds all the light in the world.

You pause a moment, imagining life
in the white farm, bread rising in a crock
by the fire, a kettle coming into song,
an oilcloth on a table laid for tea
with china cups and saucers, the door open
for sunlight to step in, or a red hen.
Voices in the yard.

You're half remembering, a cool kitchen,
a rug of sunlight on a flagstone floor.
A woman comes and goes. Your heart's in this,
but move on before the mountain takes the sun,
the white farm is returned to darkness
and the only light left anywhere
is the first star.

The Accompanist

for Wynn Thomas

So the poem speaks
from the silence of the page,
father and daughter,
piano and voice,

Hard to say who leads, who follows –
poet, composer, singer or listener,
the reader or the page,
the voice or the piano

as she sings Fauré's 'Lydia'
in a house by the sea
to the steadying sound of his hands
on the keys, the tide on the shore,

and her voice becomes bird, takes flight
and she is Lydia haunting the evening
with something like grief, like joy,
and is more than music.

Bach at St Davids

for Elin Manahan Thomas

In spring, fifteen centuries ago,
the age of saints, and stones, and holy wells,
a blackbird sang its oratorio
in the fan-vaulted canopy of the trees,
before Bach, before walls, before bells,
cantatas, choirs, cloisters, clerestories.
The audience holds its breath when the soprano,
like a bird in the forest long ago,
sings the great cathedral into being,
and apse to nave it calls back, echoing,
till orchestra and choir in harmony
break on the stones like the sea.
And listen! Out there, at the edge of spring,
among the trees, a blackbird answering.

Cattle, Hayfield, Storm

Under a black sky the trees lean seaward,
tresses blown back like figureheads
breasting an Atlantic swell.

I walk the house, a storm looming.
Over the hedge in my neighbour's mown gold field,
cattle are let in dancing, cows all colours,

a flotilla of bucking calves and a mild
blond bull, his spine a horizon, nape to tail.
None taller than he, not beast, fence, field,

not far Llanllwni mountain, not our small section
of the earth's curvature. Just a daylight moon's
above him, like the swivelling pearl of his eye.

Buffeting in from the west, a herd of squalls
shove and shoulder, kicking up a shindig.
Trees prance back from the prow of the rolling house.

The yellow field is luminous with storm-light,
cattle galumphing away ahead of the rumpus
to hunker in hedge and ditch, haunches to the storm.

The mountain stiffens its backbone before
being whelmed by a stampede of rain-storms,
and the moon shuts its one mad eye.

Gravity

Still arguing whose fault it was
after all these years,
an old sweet war to return to
those times when it ought to be perfect.
Like tonight,

when the owl cries in the garden
and we think of her heart-face,
her bloody claws.
The moon looks in through wet glass
and dissolves in tears.

You say it was all down to poetry,
the black Biba catsuit buttoned to knuckles, to throat.
I say you planned it, fetching chairs
from the empty house,
taking me back for a last look,

when you drew the bolts on the back door
and led me into the night garden,
to check the sky for Orion,
the air for that malted brew
of bonfires and Brains' Dark.

Looking up made us dizzy.
We leaned against gravity.
The planet turned a fraction
and we were done for,
falling, falling.

Wings

I wake suddenly in the night
to feel the moon's glaciers
slide their silvers over the bed
engulfing the two of us,

and touch you to be sure, scared
at the silence between the phrasing
of a breath, your shoulder cold,
your moonlit hand marble.

The early hours. I listen, lift my head
to lose the muffle of feathers,
the crack of inter-stellar static,
the knock of my own heart

and yours, beating steadily over the tundra,
paired for life, migrating through the night
in falling feathers of snow, your shoulder blades
warm again, wingless, human.

Pegging Out

As she hangs out the clothes in the rising sun
in that wild space over trees and hedges,
bed-linen billowing, putting to sea,
his shirt-arms aloft, the dawn full of gestures
as when he dressed in the morning,

she listens to the collared dove complain
from the plum tree. It occurs to her that the bird
sings to the score of the wavering blurred
illegible longhand of a high slow plane
murmuring, fly away, fly away,

over and over the same three syllables
to the beat of ripe fruit falling in the grass.

Love at Livebait

for Imtiaz and Simon

That time she stepped out of the rain
into the restaurant, and suddenly I knew.
Beautiful in her black coat,
her scarf that shocking pink
of fuchsia, geranium, wild campion,
and he at the table, his eyes her mirror.

She said she didn't know then –
but the light in her knew,
and the diners, the cutlery, the city,
the waiter filling our glasses with a soft
lloc-lloc and an updance of bubbles,
and the fish in their cradles of ice,
oceans in their eyes,

and all the colours of light in a single diamond
sliding down the window to merge with another.
Later, saying goodnight in the street,
they turned together into the city and the rain.
On the pavement one fish scale winked,
like a moon lighting half the planet.

Revival

The next revival will be a singing revival.

Joseph Parry

It was boots and hallelujahs on the roads that day.
By dawn the place was full and still they came
Under autumn skies, down steep and stony ways.
To hear a young man speak. In each a flame
Flickered in the reliquary of the heart,
Somewhere between faithlessness and hope.
We see them stilled by the camera's art,
A multitude frozen on a mountain slope,
The collier from the south driven by desire
To preach. In our dangerous century
Words can set a hungry crowd on fire,
Fists raised against the hurts of history.
What grace then, on the hill, touched those listening
And set a thousand voices singing?

Castell y Bere

Llywelyn ap Iorwerth (1173–1240)

Not hard to imagine them,
slipshod and slow on the slope to the summit,
hauling a castle up to the sky
in rain and wind, summer and winter,
stone by stone, timber by timber,
for his masons, carpenters, stone-carvers,
his craftsmen in leather and glass.
In sixty years it was over, surrendered.

Now, seven centuries on,
rain and wind, summer and winter
have scoured it of terror and blood.
All's gone to grass. What remains?
The power of a dream, his name,
and the vertebrae of a sheep –
a broken rosary dropped from the sky –
and two kites circling.

Old Libraries

Shelved quietly out of sight and mind,
The dog-eared, the foxed, the uncut, unread,
The sagging, slipped, asleep, inclined
On the shoulders of stiff volumes no one reads.
Pressed between their pages, wedding flowers,
Fingerprints, last will and testament,
Letters of longing, love, condolence,
A final note before the long descent
From a bridge over black water
Far from home in someone else's town.
And maybe once the scarcely legible lines
Of longhand like veins on the crumpled wings
Of the emerging moth, a lost sonnet soars
On one unfolded wing to the world's applause.

The Oak Wood

for Stephen Warburton (1950–2004)

Stephen, your paper slips still mark the page
in the *Cardiganshire County History*
where you noted the pollen evidence of beech
in the ancient forest, four thousand years ago.

Whenever we're out late in the wood in summer
waiting for badgers, pretending to be trees,
and the rooks come home to roost, so quiet,
one by one folding their wings like shadows,

and when we stand to go, too cold to wait,
and the whole wood breaks out in a great commotion
of woken night birds, or when we walk in the ruins
of blue, the stalks and seedheads of bluebells

turning to death and resurrection in one moment,
when the wood is holy ground dreaming cathedrals
in its columns and arcades, or when leaves turn,
and owls cry in the lofty clerestories,

you'll be there with your good counsel,
your name spoken, and on the path, your footfall.

Library Chair

er côf am John Brown (1932–2008)

*Beth yw gweithio ond gwneud cân
o'r coed a'r gwenith.*

Waldo Williams

John, before the making of my chair
You asked me for a poem. As now
I choose your chair to make my little thing of air,
The perfect pen and page, so twenty years ago,
You chose wedge and dowel, the right piece of ash
To form the lovely curve where now I lean
To think a moment, wanting the words fresh.
My fingers tell the silk-slick ebony beads
Where the sticks pierce the arm, the seat of elm.
Our songs are worked from the wood and the wheat.
Your work or mine, when art is at the helm
There's vertigo as mind and matter meet.
We leave our wake on water, in the grain of things,
With chisel or pen. Sometimes it sings.

The lines from Waldo Williams translate as: 'What is working but making a song from the wood and the wheat'.

Quayside

for Thomas Williams (1800–1888)

He was baptised in the stream at Tyddyn Shôn.
I found the place one summer afternoon
where water twisted, as it might have done,
under the bridge in a pool deep enough for a man
to drown his devils in a mountain stream,
leaving his soul caught like a rag on a stone.

from 'Cofiant', 1989

Walking by water through the gates
of castle, mountains, sky, I think of him,
great-great-grandfather, *gorhendaid*,
working the stone-boats on the Menai Straits
to the salt psalm of the sea and the wind's hymn
in the tug and thrust of the tide.
He loaded stone here on Caernarfon quay,
until he found his tongue, the chapel
his theatre, the pulpit his stage.
Words, made of breath, our chain of DNA.
Here in the new gallery the invisible angels
of language still burn in a secular age,
as if he and his kind conjured two centuries
ago a house of words by the sea.

Farewell Finisterre

One a.m., and I'm alone
with the late night announcer.
We navigate the small hours
over Viking, the Utsires, his voice
telling the island's rosary,
the stations of the night.

In the house the bottles are empty,
candles snuffed in their lighthouses,
a pulse of flame before dark fell
on the waters of Dogger, German Bight.
His words home along the airwaves.
Humber, he says, Thames, Dover, Wight.

Windows are doused one by one.
The house sleeps beyond Trafalgar, Finisterre.
The wind picks up and my heart's listening
for Lundy, Irish Sea, till words turn north,
his voice saying Shannon, Rockall,
the far away poetry of Hebrides,

and we wing out over the sea where once
from a plane travelling a latitude beyond
Fair Isle, Faroes, South East Iceland,
I saw far below the coldest word
in the school atlas. Its arctic radio name.
Its plates of ice. Its silence.

December

Cae Delyn

Midsummer, the harp-field
was strung with raked rows
silent between machines,
hay-scents rising.

Midwinter, and all growth frozen,
we find a nine-month ram
all skin and bone, too sick to run,
lost when the flock was moved.

Bring him in. Break open a bale.
Set free the locked-in summer camomiles,
vanilla, mint, wild thyme, sorrel,
wake in the creature's skull

a memory of grass,
of flock and field,
of being alive.

Advent

Dark times. December.
Earth's axis on the slant
and the minutes fall from the day
a few at a time.

So we outsleep the dark,
sleepwalking the grey hours.
Impossible to believe in light,
or a birth, until

this winter sunrise, fox
going home with blood in its mouth,
all the dawn's chemicals in its eye,
and the sky astonished.

The Darkest Day

Even in the dead of winter,
the nights long, the days twilit,
comes a moment when clouds break
for a cold, invisible sun.

Then the sea brings home its cargo,
the stones release their metals
and a startle of sun fires pool and puddle
till every rivulet of gold

is Nile, Tigris, Euphrates, Jordan,
uttering light.

Solstice

We feast in the darkest night
at the midnight of the year
brazening out the narrowing days with light.

Out there in our temperate city
an ice rink glitters on a civic lawn
as if we dreamed Victorian glitter

when lakes were dancing floors,
the rivers froze for goose fairs
and all was marble winter out of doors.

For now, let the city put on party clothes.
Dress every tree with electricity.
Switch on the lights. Let streets and houses glow.

When the party's over, and we step into the night,
maybe the Ice Queen's wand, an imagined
hush of snow, will touch the heart,

and we'll know, for the pleasures of here and now,
we are borrowing bling from the glacier, slipping
Greenland's shoulder from its wrap of snow.

Dawn

A dark swish of starlings
like curtains parting
in a hushed auditorium

and the show begins:
a bowl of fire in a beech tree,
then earth and sky suffused in flame.

This could be the first dawn,
the world brand new,
just out of its wrapper,

sky a great window open
a moment only
in the east,

giving a glimpse of the myth
before the first footprint,
before the fall.

Shepherd

Christmas, and over the snow
a jet chases the day,
cresting the sill of the land
to take the Atlantic.

In the fields
a man and his dog
check the sheep dawn and dusk
as they've always done.

What's it to him,
the flight of kings,
but to remind him
that the world turns,

that going home is a prayer,
that even war draws breath.